SCIENCE CORNER

Push and Pull

Angela Royston

Explore the world with **Popcorn** - your complete first non-fiction library.

Look out for more titles in the **Popcorn** range. All books have the same format of simple text and vibrant images. Text is carefully matched to the pictures to help readers to identify and understand key vocabulary.
www.waylandbooks.co.uk/popcorn

Published in 2012 by Wayland

Wayland
338 Euston Road
London NW1 3BH

Wayland Australia
Level 17/207 Kent Street
Sydney NSW 2000

Editor: Katie Powell
Designer: Robert Walster
Picture Researcher: Diana Morris

British Library Cataloguing in Publication Data
 Royston, Angela.
   Push and pull. -- (Popcorn. Science corner)
   1. Force and energy--Juvenile literature.
   I. Title II. Series
   531.1'1-dc22
 ISBN 978 0 7502 6437 2

First published in 2010 by Wayland
Copyright © Wayland 2010

This paperback edition published in 2010 by Wayland
Reprinted by Wayland in 2011 and 2012
Printed and bound in China

Wayland is a division of Hachette Children's Books,
an Hachette UK Company.
www.hachette.co.uk

Photographs:
Don Bayley/istockphoto: 17. John Bloor/istockphoto: 2, 8. Bronwyn photo/istockphoto: 16. Christian Carrol/istockphoto: 10. Rob Friedman/istockphoto: 15. Juice Images/Alamy: 6. Herbert Kim/istockphoto: 21. Paul Kline/istockphoto: 14. Josef Muellek/istockphoto: 1, 18. Catalin Petolea/Shutterstock: 7. Pixland/Corbis: 11. Eve Serrabassa/istockphoto: 19. Steve Shepard/istockphoto: 4. Jacoms Stephens/istockphoto: 9. Steve Stone/istockphoto: 12. Leah-Anne Thompson/istockphoto: front cover, 13. Valenty/istockphoto: 20. Wayland: 22, 23. Artmann Witt/istockphoto: 5.

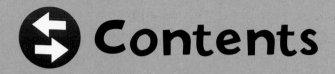 # Contents

Pushing and pulling   4

Pushes   6

Pulls   8

How things move   10

Making things move faster   12

Changing direction   14

Slowing things down   16

Force of the wind   18

Moving water   20

Car chase   22

Glossary   24

Index   24

Pushing and pulling

Pushing and pulling are both forces.
Some forces are small. It only takes
a small force to push a toy truck.

Other forces are big. It takes a big force to push a heavy car.

 # Pushes

A push sends something away from you. You push a supermarket trolley to make it move.

Sometimes you push with your hands and arms. But you have to push with your foot when you ride a scooter.

When you kick a ball, you push it with your foot.

 # Pulls

A pull brings something towards you.
For example, you pull open a drawer.

Wheels make it easier to pull
all sorts of things. Most suitcases
have wheels to make them easy
to pull.

How things move

When you are on a swing, you move forwards and backwards. A seesaw moves up and down.

Other things move in a circle. You turn
the pedals of a bicycle to make the
wheels go round.

A roundabout moves around in a circle.

Making things move faster

A force can make something move faster. The harder you push the pedals of a bike, the faster the bike moves.

The harder you push a toy car,
the faster it moves. When you stop
pushing, the car slows down.

Changing direction

Pushing and pulling can make something change direction. This dog is on a lead. The owner pulls the lead to make the dog change direction.

When you hit a ball with a bat,
the ball changes direction. The ball
stops coming towards you and
spins away from you instead.

Slowing things down

A force can slow down or stop something that is moving. When you catch a ball, you stop it moving.

Warning! Don't try to stop something heavy. It could knock you over.

Bicycles, cars and other vehicles all have brakes to make them slow down. A brake pushes a block against the wheel to slow the wheel down.

wheel

brake block

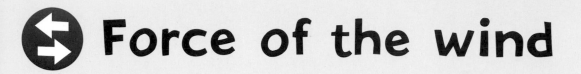# Force of the wind

Wind is moving air. The faster the air moves, the stronger the wind. When you fly a kite, the force of the wind lifts the kite into the air.

18

Wind is a natural force, because it is not made by people. People can use natural forces to work machines.

The force of the wind turns the blades of a wind turbine to make electricity.

Moving water

Moving water is also a natural force. Water runs downhill into streams and rivers.

The water can push along leaves, twigs and logs.

Waves are moving water. Big waves hit the shore with a huge force.

Car chase

Try this simple experiment to discover more about the force of pushing.

1. Mark a cross on a piece of black paper with the chalk.

2. Put the car on the cross and push it as hard as you can with your finger.

3. Measure how far the car goes.

4. Ask your friend to have a go. Make sure they start from the same point.

5. Measure how far the car goes.

Who pushed the car the furthest?

Who used the most force?

Glossary

brake a device for making a bicycle, car or other vehicle slow down or stop

direction the place that something is heading towards

electricity a form of energy that is used to work some machines

force something that makes a thing move, or changes the way it is moving

machine a device made by people to do a particular thing

natural something that is made by nature

pedal the part of a machine that you push with your foot to make something move

vehicle a machine that carries people and things from one place to another

Index

backwards 10

bicycle 11, 12, 17

brake 17

car 5, 17

circle 11

down 10

electricity 19

fast 12-13, 18

force 4, 5, 12, 16, 18-19, 20, 21, 22, 23

forwards 10

pulls 4-5, 8-9, 14

push 4-5, 6-7, 12, 13, 14, 17, 20, 22, 23

slow 13, 16, 17

up 10

vehicles 17

water 20-21

waves 21

wheels 9, 11, 17

wind 18-19

wind turbine 19